Celebrating American Holidays
CINCO
DE MAYO

Leia Tait and Jordan McGill

www.av2books.com

AV² provides enriched content that supplements and complements this book. Weigl's AV² books strive to create inspired learning and engage young minds in a total learning experience.

Your AV² Media Enhanced books come alive with...

Audio
Listen to sections of the book read aloud.

Key Words
Study vocabulary, and complete a matching word activity.

Go to **www.av2books.com**, and enter this book's unique code.

Video
Watch informative video clips.

Quizzes
Test your knowledge.

BOOK CODE

T551090

Embedded Weblinks
Gain additional information for research.

Slide Show
View images and captions, and prepare a presentation.

AV² by Weigl brings you media enhanced books that support active learning.

Try This!
Complete activities and hands-on experiments.

... and much, much more!

Published by Weigl Publishers Inc.
350 5th Avenue, 59th Floor
New York, NY 10118
Website: www.weigl.com

Library of Congress Cataloging-in-Publication Data

Cinco de Mayo / edited by Jordan McGill.
    p. cm. -- (Celebrating American holidays: Arts & crafts)
 ISBN 978-1-61690-682-5 (hardcover : alk. paper) -- ISBN 978-1-61690-688-7 (softcover : alk. paper)
 1. Cinco de Mayo (Mexican holiday)--Juvenile literature. 2. Mexico--Social life and customs--Juvenile literature. 3. Cinco de Mayo, Battle of, Puebla, Mexico, 1862--Juvenile literature. I. McGill, Jordan.
 F1233.C58 2012
 394.262--dc22
                             2011002428

Printed in the United States of America in North Mankato, Minnesota
1 2 3 4 5 6 7 8 9 0 15 14 13 12 11

062011
WEP180511

Project Coordinator Jordan McGill   **Art Director** Terry Paulhus

Every reasonable effort has been made to trace ownership and to obtain permission to reprint copyright material. The publishers would be pleased to have any errors or omissions brought to their attention so that they may be corrected in subsequent printings.

Weigl acknowledges Getty Images as its primary image supplier for this title. Craft photos by Madison Helton.

CONTENTS

6

10

14

20

What is Cinco de Mayo?

Every year on May 5, Cinco de Mayo is celebrated across Mexico and the United States. Cinco de Mayo is Spanish for "the fifth of May." This holiday celebrates the **victory** of the Mexican army over the French at *La Batalla de Puebla*, or the Battle of Puebla, in 1862. Mexicans and Mexican Americans began celebrating this holiday more than 100 years ago. Today, Cinco de Mayo is a national holiday in Mexico and the United States.

On Cinco de Mayo, people find many exciting ways to celebrate Mexican culture. Crowds gather in city streets to hear lively music. They join in parades and watch colorful dance shows. Tasty foods are made just for the event. Children dress in festive costumes and perform **traditional** songs and dances. People decorate their homes and public buildings with bright flowers and Mexican flags.

History of Cinco de Mayo

In 1861, Mexico owed money to many countries. Mexico asked the rulers of Great Britain, Spain, and France for two years to repay its debts. Only Great Britain and Spain agreed. France wanted to take control of all of Mexico. It sent its army to conquer Mexico.

The Mexican people formed an army to fight the French, but most of the men had no military training. The United States helped Mexico prepare for the fight. It gave Mexico weapons for the battle. Some Americans even joined the Mexican army.

The two armies met near the city of Puebla on May 5, 1862. After four hours of fighting, Mexico won the battle. *El Cinco de Mayo*, or "the fifth of May," became a **symbol** of Mexican strength and **unity**.

Wish for a Milagro

A milagro is a Mexican good luck charm. The word milagro means "miracle." People use milagros to ask or to give thanks for favors, such as victory in battle.

What You Need

- pencil
- paper
- gel markers
- glitter
- modeling clay
- glue
- aluminum foil

5 Easy Steps to Make Your Milagro

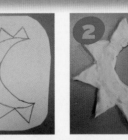

1 Draw a plan for your milagro. What kind of shape or object do you think will bring you good luck?

2 Use the modeling clay to create the shape of your milagro.

3 Wrap aluminum foil around the shape of the clay. Glue the ends to keep the foil in place.

4 Decorate your milagro using markers and glitter.

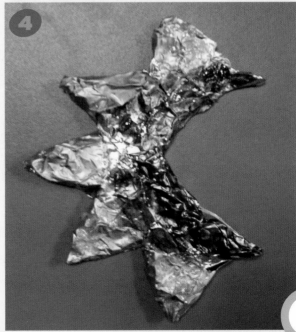

5 Carry your milagro with you for good luck!

A Mexican Hero

General Ignacio Zaragoza led the Mexican army at the Battle of Puebla. General Zaragoza had been born and raised in Mexico. He did not want France to conquer his country.

Before the battle began, General Zaragoza gave a speech. He told his people that even though the French army was strong, Mexico could win the battle. His words cheered the Mexican soldiers. They felt ready to fight.

Draw General Zaragoza

Use the picture on the right to draw a portrait of General Zaragoza.

What You Need

- drawing paper
- pencil
- crayons or markers
- eraser

8 Easy Steps to Complete Your Drawing

1 Draw an oval on the paper that is taller than it is wide. This will be General Zaragoza's face.

2 Lightly draw a cross through the middle of the oval. These two lines will help you place General Zaragoza's features on his face.

3 Draw General Zaragoza's mouth between the horizontal line and the bottom of the oval.

4 To make the general's nose, draw two small circles on each side of the vertical center line. They should be placed between the mouth and the horizontal center line. These small circles will be his nostrils. Use them as a guide to draw the complete nose.

5 General Zaragoza's eyes will be placed on the top half of the oval. Draw one eye on each side of the vertical center line.

6 Now you should have the outline of General Zaragoza's face. To make your drawing look like Zaragoza, add ears, eyebrows, and hair. The tops of his ears should be level with his eyes. For basic ears, draw a "C" on each side of Zaragoza's head.

7 To add General Zaragoza's glasses, draw ovals around his eyes. Connect these ovals together with a line across Zaragoza's nose. Then, draw lines going to his ears.

8 Use markers or pencil crayons to color your portrait of General Zaragoza.

Celebrating Today

Cinco de Mayo is a chance for people to have fun and learn about Mexican **culture**. The holiday is often celebrated with a **fiesta**. At the fiesta, people can eat Mexican food and listen or dance to Mexican music. Some people perform the *jarabe tapatio*, or Mexican Hat Dance. It is the national dance of Mexico.

Many Cinco de Mayo celebrations include carnivals and fairs. People play games and buy crafts. Parades with brightly colored floats wind through the streets.

Shake a Maraca

Maracas are a type of rattle that people use to play Mexican music.

What You Need

- two paper plates
- dried beans, rice, or hard popcorn
- glue
- one popsicle stick
- markers, paint, glitter, or crayons

5 Easy Steps to Make Your Maraca

1. Decorate the outside of the plates using markers, paint, glitter, or crayons. If you use paint or glitter, let your decorations dry before continuing.

2. Lay one of the plates on a flat surface, with the inside facing up. Place a handful of beans, rice, or popcorn on the inside of the plate.

3. Apply glue to the rim of the plate. Place the other plate on top of the plate containing the beans, rice, or popcorn.

4. Before the glue dries, place part of the popsicle stick in between the two plates. Leave enough of the stick outside of the plates so that you have a handle for your maraca. Press the edges of the plates together to set the glue. Leave to dry.

5. Once the glue is dry, shake your maraca, and make some noise.

Mexican Flag

Mexico's flag is made up of three bands of color. Green is on the left, white is in the middle, and red is on the right. Each color has a special meaning. The green band represents independence. The white band symbolizes **religion**. The red band stands for unity. At Cinco de Mayo festivals, these colors can be seen everywhere.

The flag's white band holds a picture of an eagle with a snake in its beak. Legend says that the gods told the **Aztec** people to build a city where they saw an eagle and a snake. This is now Mexico City.

Wave a Flag

Follow these instructions to make your own Mexican flag to wave on Cinco de Mayo.

What You Need

- white, red, and green paper
- scissors
- glue
- crayons or markers
- stick
- ruler

5 Easy Steps to Complete Your Flag

1 Before you start, make sure that all the pieces of paper are the same size.

2 Take the green paper, and place it lengthwise in front of you. Use the ruler to measure 1/3 of the paper. Fold the paper along this line, and then cut it.

3 Do the same with the red paper.

4 Take the white paper, and place it in front of you so that it is greater in length than height. Glue the green paper onto the left third of the white paper. Do the same with the red paper on the right side. Leave the middle white.

5 In the center of the white section, draw an eagle holding a snake with its mouth and feet. Draw curved rows of flowers under the eagle to match the image on this page.

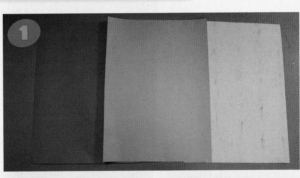

Fireworks

Most Mexican fiestas begin with the sound of *fuegos artificiales*, or fireworks, exploding in the sky. Fireworks signal that something special is about to begin.

On Cinco de Mayo, fireworks light up the sky a second time after dark. Just like on the Fourth of July, they signal a happy end to a day of celebrating.

Paint a Fireworks Display

What do you see when fireworks light the sky? Paint a picture of the colorful scene.

What You Need

- water
- sugar
- a small bowl
- colored chalk
- black construction paper

6 Easy Steps to Paint Your Display

1. Fill the bowl with warm water.

2. Add sugar to the water until the sugar stops dissolving. Stir the water. The water should become thick.

3. Dip the colored chalk into the water.

4. Draw lines with the chalk on the black paper. At the top ends of the lines, draw bursts going in many directions.

5. Let the chalk dry. The water will evaporate, leaving only sparkling fireworks.

6. When the picture is dry, display it on your fridge or a wall.

Piñatas

Piñatas are **papier-mâché** containers filled with treats. The containers are often made in the shapes of animals. The Spanish brought piñatas to Mexico nearly 400 years ago.

During a fiesta, a piñata is hung from a tree. Children are blindfolded, and they take turns trying to break the piñata with a stick. The parents move the piñata up and down with a rope. When the piñata breaks, treats spill out, and the children pick up the prizes.

Make a Piñata

What You Need

- scissors
- bowl
- 1 balloon
- 6 to 8 cups of water
- paint

- 3 to 4 cups of flour
- masking tape
- newspaper
- scrap paper
- party hats

5 Easy Steps to Complete Your Piñata

1 Use scissors to cut the newspaper into long strips.

2 Pour 1 cup of flour and 2 cups of water into the bowl. Mix it together using a spoon.

3 Blow up the balloon. Tie the balloon so that no air escapes.

4 Dip the strips of newspaper into the flour and water mixture. Place them all over the balloon so that it is completely covered.

5 When the strips have dried, attach the party hats and scraps of paper. Paint the piñata to make it colorful.

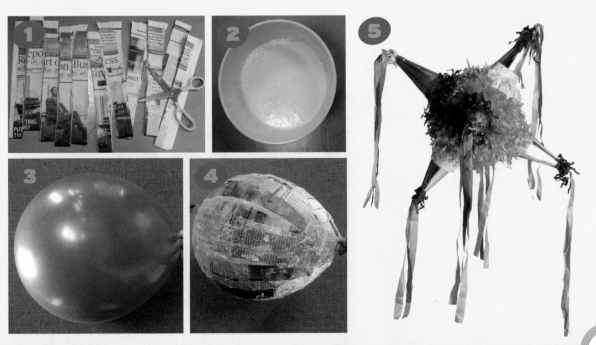

A Song to Remember

Music is an important part of Cinco de Mayo. People sometimes sing Mexican folk songs. One such song is "*De colores.*" "*De colores*" is a traditional Mexican song. It means "All the Colors" in English. This is part of the English translation of the song.

All the colors, all the colors, oh how they dress up the countryside in springtime,

All the colors, all the colors of birdies, oh how they come back to us outside,

All the colors, all the colors in rainbows we see shining bright in the sky,

And that's why a great love of the colors makes me feel like singing so joyfully,

And that's why a great love of the colors makes me feel like singing so joyfully.

The rooster sings, he sings cock-a-doodle, doodle, doodle, doodle, doodle, doodle, doodle-doo,

The chicken clucks, she clucks, cluck, cluck, cluck, cluck, cluck, cluck, cluck, cluck, cluck, cluck, cluck, cluck,

The little chicks they cheep, they cheep, cheep, cheep, cheep, cheep, cheep, cheep, cheep, cheep, cheep, cheep, cheep, cheep, cheep,

And that's why a great love of the colors makes me feel like singing so joyfully,

And that's why a great love of the colors makes me feel like singing so joyfully.

18

Write a Song

Write your own Cinco de Mayo song lyrics using the chart below and the words at the bottom of the page. How many Cinco de Mayo words can you use in your Cinco de Mayo song?

Get some friends to write their own songs, and sing them aloud.

1 Start brainstorming ideas. What do you want your song to be about? Choose an event, idea, person, or feeling you would like to write about.

2 Many songs have a chorus. The chorus is the main idea of the song. It connects the verses and is repeated several times.

The "All the Colors" chorus begins

"And that's why a great love of the colors makes me feel like singing so joyfully."

3 Write the verses. Songs usually have three to four verses. Each one will be different, but all should relate to the chorus.

The final verse ends the song.

4 Once you have written your song, read over the lyrics again. Are there any changes you could make to improve the song? "All the Colors," repeats similar phrases at the beginning of several lines. For example, the first three lines start "All the colors, all the colors," and later, each line begins with an animal and follows with the sounds it makes.

Cinco de Mayo Words to Use

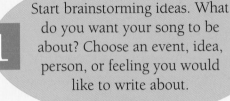

maraca   cinco de mayo   flag   strength   flowers   general

piñatas   chocolate   ignacio zaragoza   floats   Mexico

fireworks   mexican   fiesta   battle   crowds   mariachi

Cinco de Mayo Foods

Cinco de Mayo is a day to make and eat Mexican food. Corn, beans, rice, chocolate, avocado, cheese, and spicy peppers are common ingredients in Mexican foods. Popular Mexican foods include gorditas and buñuelos.

Chocolate is used in both drinks and dishes, and not only for dessert. Mexican hot chocolate is traditionally made twice a day, all year round. Mole, a kind of sauce, is made by grinding chiles, nuts, vegetables, spices, and chocolate together. The sauce can be poured over turkey or chicken.

Mexican Hot Chocolate

Make this warm drink on a cold day!

What You Need

- 2 ounces unsweetened chocolate
- 2 cups milk
- 1 cup heavy cream
- 6 tablespoons sugar
- 1/2 teaspoon cinnamon

5 Easy Steps to Make Your Hot Chocolate

1. With an adult's help, melt the chocolate in a saucepan.

2. In a pot, warm the milk and cream on a low heat until hot. Do not burn the liquid.

3. Add a bit of hot milk to the melted chocolate, and mix to form a paste.

4. Then, stir in the remaining milk mixture, sugar, and cinnamon.

5. Serve and enjoy.

What Have You Learned?

1 What does Cinco de Mayo mean?

2 What event does Cinco de Mayo celebrate?

3 Who led the Mexican army at the Battle of Puebla?

4 What are the colors of the Mexican flag, and what do they mean?

5 What animals are featured in the center of the Mexican flag?

6 What is a piñata?

7 What do many Mexicans drink twice each day?

Quiz Answers: 1. Cinco de Mayo means "fifth of May" in Spanish. This is the day that the holiday takes place. 2. Cinco de Mayo celebrates the victory of the Mexican army over the French at the Battle of Puebla. 3. General Ignacio Zaragoza led the army. 4. The colors on the Mexican flag are green, white, and red. Green stands for independence, white for religion, and red for unity. 5. An eagle and a snake are featured in the center of the Mexican flag. 6. A piñata is a papier mâché container filled with treats. 7. Many Mexicans drink Mexican hot chocolate twice each day.

Glossary

Aztec: people who once lived in central Mexico

culture: the habits and customs of groups of people

fiesta: a festival or celebration

papier-mâché: shreds of paper mixed with glue or paste

religion: a system of belief

symbol: something that stands for something else

traditional: of or related to history

unity: the state of being together

victory: success over an enemy

Index

Log on to www.av2books.com

AV² by Weigl brings you media enhanced books that support active learning. Go to www.av2books.com, and enter the special code found on page 2 of this book. You will gain access to enriched and enhanced content that supplements and complements this book. Content includes video, audio, web links, quizzes, a slide show, and activities.

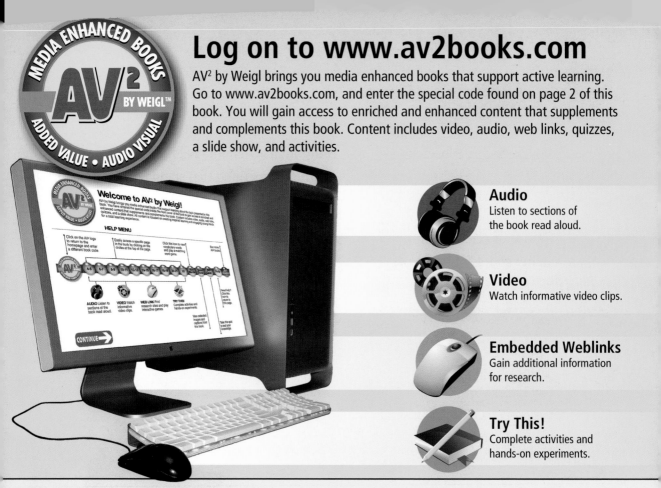

Audio
Listen to sections of the book read aloud.

Video
Watch informative video clips.

Embedded Weblinks
Gain additional information for research.

Try This!
Complete activities and hands-on experiments.

WHAT'S ONLINE?

Try This!	Embedded Weblinks	Video	EXTRA FEATURES
Try more fun activities.	Find out more about the history of Cinco de Mayo.	Watch a video about Cinco de Mayo.	**Audio** Listen to sections of the book read aloud.
Write a biography about an important person.	Find out more about an important holiday symbol.	Check out another video about Cinco de Mayo.	**Key Words** Study vocabulary, and complete a matching word activity.
Make another recipe.	Read more information about Cinco de Mayo.		**Slide Show** View images and captions, and prepare a presentation.
Play an interactive activity.	Find out about a similar celebration.		**Quizzes** Test your knowledge.

AV² was built to bridge the gap between print and digital. We encourage you to tell us what you like and what you want to see in the future.
Sign up to be an AV² Ambassador at www.av2books.com/ambassador.